Victory Journal

VICTORY
JOURNAL

*TO YOUR
HEART'S DESIRE*

LESLIE JACKSON

Victory Journal: to Your Heart's Desire
Copyright © 2023 Leslie Jackson

All Rights Reserved. No part of this book may be reproduced in any form or by any means, electronic, or mechanical, including photography, recording, e-books, or any information storage and retrieval system, without permission in writing from the publisher.

ISBN: 978-1-7345854-5-2

Book Design by Paul Nylander | Illustrada

Printed in the United States of America

For information:
https://LeslieJackson.org
Leslie@LeslieJackson.org

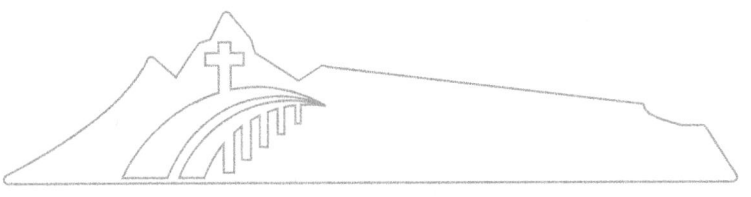

Table of Contents

Introduction   1

1—What's your Story?   3
2—Masks & Make-up   9
3—Shaped, Not Defined   17
4—Grieving Loss and Celebrating Love   25
5—Looking for Love   35
6—Parenting Joys   45
7—Health & Addiction: Choosing Life   53
8—Believing is Seeing   61
9—Finding Purpose and Dreaming Again   71
10—Embracing Adventure   77

Conclusion   83
Author's note to all readers   85

"Do not despise these small beginnings, for the LORD rejoices to see the work begin,"
(Zechariah 4:10a NLT)

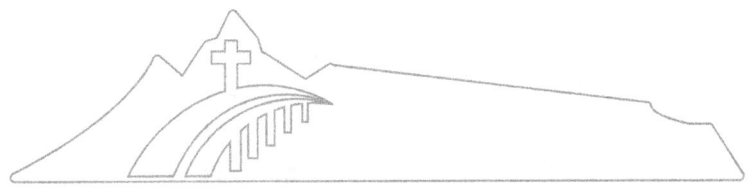

Introduction

This book was created after *Change Course; One Lady's Race from Acceptance to Adventure*, Leslie Jackson's memoire, to guide others through a life changing experience of renewal and restoration, similar to what Leslie experienced.

This book is intentionally small so you can bring it with you and meditate on its contents. Go through this book and journal as often as you need to remove any hurt, pain, shame, or regrets that are in the way of living out your heart's desire. Feel free to also grab a notebook and make notes in it. You can burn the pages from your notebook after you have healed from the past and are ready to move on and live out God's purpose for your life.

Victory Journal

As you travel through this journal, I pray you feel the love of God and receive His wisdom and guidance, day by day.

Now, let's get started, as we do this together with God our Father!

> *"Jesus looked at them intently and said,*
> *'Humanly speaking, it is impossible.*
> *But with God everything is possible.'"*
> (Matthew 19:26 NLT)

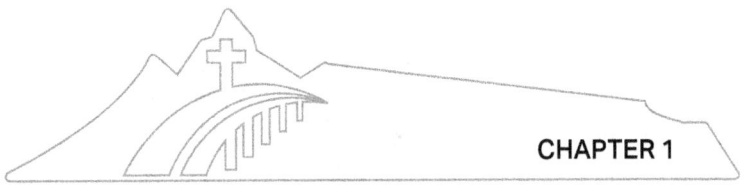

CHAPTER 1

What's your Story?

*"Everyone will share the story of your
wonderful goodness; they will sing
with joy about your righteousness."*
(Psalm 145:7 NLT)

In Chapter 1 of my book *Change Course*, I tell about my experience of the first telling of my story. It was nerve-wracking to put myself out there, but in the end, it gave me power and healing, and became the catalyst for writing my books. The first telling of your story may be nerve-wracking too. It can be hard to be open and vulnerable. But when it is done in a safe environment, it is very freeing and liberating.

Victory Journal

In this chapter, you will begin the process of telling your story. You can pick a part of your story to tell and maybe tell other parts later.

What's your Story?

EXERCISES

Think of a time in your life when something happened that had a profound effect on you. It can be a big or small event but should be something that means a lot to you. List 2–3 events in your life that were "life changing" and note them briefly here.

1. _____

2. _____

3. _____

Pick one of these events that impacted you the most and write out the details.

_____
_____
_____
_____
_____

Victory Journal

Now that you have written out part of your story, you get to tell it to someone. Who do you know is a trusted friend, full of love, compassion, and a good listener? Arrange to meet with that person so you can tell the story you just wrote down.

How did you feel after accomplishing the task of telling a part of your story?

What's your Story?

BEYOND THE FINISH LINE

Now that you have experienced writing and telling part of your story, keep going! Tell another part of your story, and then another, and maybe even another. You never know, you might end up with a book, or a podcast.

When we tell our story, we help others tell theirs. Who can you help encourage the first telling of their story? Write that person's name down and reach out to them.

Who knows, you might be the inspiration for someone to start living out their own heart's desire?

Victory Journal

THE GOD STORY
God lovingly crafted a beautiful story, purpose for your life. Let's take a minute to thank Him for it.

Dear God,

Thank you for the story you wrote for me. I thank you that my story is not over yet, and You have more for me. I trust that your love and grace will provide the perfect ending.

Amen.

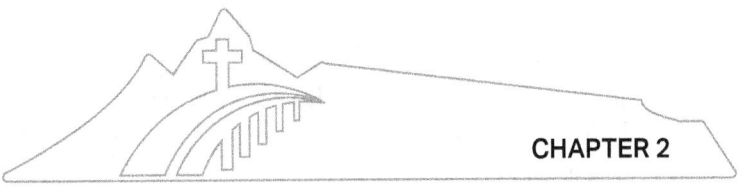

CHAPTER 2

Masks & Make-up

> *"You made all the delicate, inner parts
> of my body and knit me together in my
> mother's womb. Thank you for making me
> so wonderfully complex! Your workmanship
> is marvelous—how well I know it."*
> (Psalm 139:13–14 NLT)

In Chapter 2 of my book *Change Course*, I share the story of the rare skin disease that left me with spots all over my body. People would stare and point and pull their kids away from me at the swimming pool. I even wrote a song, "Please don't hurt my little girl," that I would sing to comfort myself, usually when I was alone in the bathroom.

Victory Journal

Later, I used make-up, long sleeves, and long pants to hide the spots. We all hide behind something to cover up those things we don't want anyone to know about. Sometimes it's make-up, sometimes it's a mask, pretending to be someone we're not. These behaviors usually stem from the lies we believe about ourselves.

It took me a long time to rebuild my self-esteem from the damage caused when I was a young girl and get to the point of self-acceptance, but I did it, and you can too! A big part of getting to that point has been embracing God's love for me, knowing He made me perfect, just how He wanted me to be; height, fingerprints, ear shape, etc. . . . because I'm perfectly His. This is the truth I had to use to combat the lies I had previously believed.

In this chapter of the book, you will go through an exercise in self-image. By the end of this exercise, I hope you are one step closer to seeing yourself as the beautiful creation you are!

Masks & Make-up

EXERCISES

Make a list of seven attributes about yourself (stated by others). They can be internal or external, positive, or negative, truthful, or a lie.

1. _____
2. _____
3. _____
4. _____
5. _____
6. _____
7. _____

Now go back to each one and write down how you received that message about yourself (at school, a party, work, etc.).

Now that you have your list, go back to each one and right next to it, TRUTH or LIE (did this person say this to you out of fear, anger, hatred, confusion, love, compassion, etc. Meditating on this will help determine if it is a TRUTH or LIE).

Victory Journal

Go back to any attributes you labeled, "LIE." How have these lies impacted the way you look at yourself? After this meditation, seek guidance from the Lord to help you release these lies and receive the endless love that the Lord has for you in place of those lies.

Go back to any attributes you labeled, "TRUTH." How have these truths impacted the way you look at yourself?

Masks & Make-up

The Bible verse at the beginning of this chapter says that God "knit" or crafted every part of you, hidden and seen, and that He made you "wonderfully complex." When you think about God creating you uniquely because He loves you, how does that impact the way you look at yourself?

_____

_____

_____

_____

_____

_____

_____

Set a goal to say something positive about how God made you or compliment yourself on something each day. These steps will help to reframe your view of yourself, improve your self-esteem, and lead you towards self-acceptance.

Victory Journal

BEYOND THE FINISH LINE

Improving your self-esteem and getting to self-acceptance can feel like a long race. You may need to retrain your brain on what an amazing job God did when He made you. Don't give up! Keep coming back to this exercise whenever your self-esteem takes a nose-dive, and you find yourself hiding behind masks or make-up.

Masks & Make-up

GOD BROKE THE MOLD
God broke the mold when He made you, literally. There is not another you! Take a moment to thank God for how He created you.

Dear God,

Thank you for crafting me together the way you did. You broke the mold when you made me and created each aspect of me with love and purpose. I give you thanks and praise for your beautiful creation. Please help me to see how wonderfully complex I am.

Amen

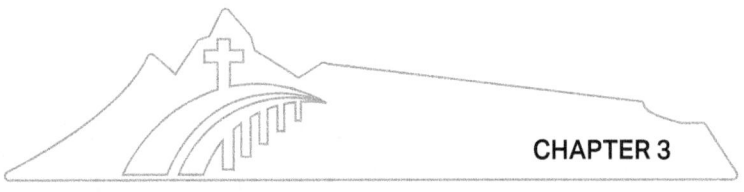

CHAPTER 3

Shaped, Not Defined

> *"Our past may shape us, but it doesn't define who we become."*
> *– Alyson Noel*

In Chapter 3 of my book *Change Course*, I talk about my childhood and the changes that occurred in my family. My parents divorced when my father left my mother for another woman (my friend's mom). Then my mother married the ex-husband of my father's new wife. I call this Parent Swap. This shaped me in many ways, but so did other things. I had an absent father, but a very present and loving grandfather. I gained several siblings who were previously my friends. Also, my mom and stepdad fostered many foster children in our home.

Victory Journal

Some of my early family experiences shaped me negatively and some shaped me positively. But they all shaped me. They shaped me, but they didn't define me. There is a difference. And understanding that difference is important.

Every part of our lives is woven together by a loving God. Nothing that happens to us is a surprise to Him. He can use every bit and piece of our functional and dysfunctional family for good in our lives. It may not always look good when it happens, but hindsight can be a good teacher. I remind myself often; With God, all things are possible.

In this chapter, you will go through an exercise that will highlight defining moments or milestones in your early life. On the other side of this exercise, my hope is that you too will be able to see the good that was shaped in you through these events and how God is still using them today to show you His great love for you.

Shaped, Not Defined

EXERCISES

In each of the following segments of your life, write down defining moments, major milestones, or relational changes and influences from your life. There's no need to get specific, just a statement or phrase that describes the events or changes.

Birth to 5 Years

Elementary School

Middle School/Junior High

High School Years

Early 20's

Victory Journal

Look back at your list of milestones and underline each event that had a negative impact on you. Then circle each event that had a positive impact on you.

Pick one of the milestones of your life and describe how it has shaped you.

_____

_____

_____

Pick one of the milestones of your life and describe how you have allowed it to define you.

_____

_____

_____

"Flip the script"—Take a negative defining statement and make it into a positive shaping statement. State it here.

_____

_____

_____

_____

Shaped, Not Defined

Going through this exercise will most likely make the past come "calling." However, you won't want the past to keep calling after you have put it into the proper perspective. Limit the amount of time the past gets, so you don't get stuck in a lengthy conversation with it.

Victory Journal

BEYOND THE FINISH LINE

Looking back at past events of our childhoods can be heavy work. This isn't a "one and done" type of exercise. As you keep pressing towards the life you want, you may need to go back to each of those milestones and process through the questions and reflection exercises in this chapter. If you don't do the work on this, those milestones can turn into heavy stones (a.k.a. millstone) that weigh you down, turning them into hazards on the road to your new life. Celebrate where you have been and what you learned from those experiences as they propel you to your future victory.

Shaped, Not Defined

GOD'S TIMELINE

God lovingly holds you through every part of your life, even when you don't realize it. Take a few minutes to thank Him for His love during the good and challenging parts of your life.

Dear God,

Thank you for my life and the ways it has shaped me into the person I am today. There are some parts of it that I don't understand, and others that make me smile. I am thankful for your hand in my life story and that you have been with me every step of the way, even when I didn't see you. I'm thankful that you can use even the bad and challenging things for good. I'm excited to see the beauty you have lovingly planned for me in the future.

Amen.

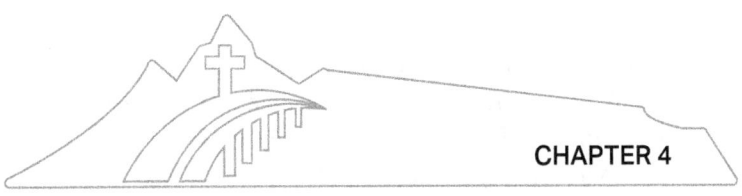

CHAPTER 4

Grieving Loss and Celebrating Love

> *"The Lord is my rock, my fortress, and my savior; my God is my rock, in whom I find protection. He is my shield, the power that saves me, and my place of safety."*
> (Psalm 18:2 NLT)

In Chapter 4 of my book *Change Course,* I share the painful life event of my brother Scott dying unexpectedly in a car accident. His death changed our lives forever and his memory is still alive within us today. There are losses in our lives other than the death of a loved one who is precious to us. Shortly after my brother died, we moved to Ohio, and I no longer was able to see my dear Grandpa with whom I was very close.

Victory Journal

Later during my divorces, I struggled with the loss of those relationships. My mind had negative chatter on replay that needed to be shut down. Eventually I was able to forgive my ex-husbands and forgive myself for the part I played in the divorces and accept God's love and forgiveness.

In this chapter you will identify areas of loss in your life and learn a few ways to grieve those losses. You will also identify key relationships in your life and learn how to celebrate them.

Grieving Loss and Celebrating Love

EXERCISES

Grieving Loss

Which of the following losses have you experienced? Circle all that apply.

Death of a parent	Financial loss
Death of a spouse	Loss of a job
Death of a child	Loss of a friendship
Death of a friend	Divorce
Death of a sibling	Bankruptcy
Chronic disease or illness	Foreclosure
	Moving to a new place

Other: _____

Other: _____

Victory Journal

Of all the losses you circled, which one has proved the hardest in processing your grief?

Of the losses you circled, are there any you hadn't really considered a loss to grieve until now? Why or why not?

Take one of the losses you circled and answer the following questions:

Which of the losses listed in question #1 do you miss the most and why?

Grieving Loss and Celebrating Love

What would your life look like today if that loss hadn't occurred?

What is better in your life now because that loss occurred? (Looking for the positive in a hard situation.)

These questions can reveal a lot about how you have processed and persevered through loss.

As you look at your answers to the questions, what stands out to you that you never noticed before?

Victory Journal

Celebrating Love

List below the names and roles of every key love relationship in your life, whether or not they are still in your life today.

___

___

___

___

Think about two people that you would like to celebrate. For each, answer the following questions:

Why is this person a key love relationship in my life?

___

___

___

___

___

___

___

Grieving Loss and Celebrating Love

How has this person helped make my life better?

How have I helped make this person's life better?

How can I celebrate this person to show gratitude for their love?

BEYOND THE FINISH LINE
If you need to do some more exploring of your losses and loves so you can change course and live the life you want, go back, and complete the questions for all your losses (or even just one more). And/or go back and pick a few more key love relationships to celebrate.

Grieving Loss and Celebrating Love

GOD'S GIFTS

In the Bible, there was a man named Job who lost everything, I mean EVERYTHING! After he lost all 10 of his children in one day, he said the words quoted below. In essence, Job thanks God for both the giving and the taking away.

> *"He said, 'I came naked from my mother's womb, and I will be naked when I leave. The LORD gave me what I had, and the LORD has taken it away. Praise the name of the LORD!'"* (Job 1:21 NLT)

The entire story of Job is fascinating. I encourage you to read and meditate upon the story and on how Satan spoke to God and how Job's friends said many hurtful, incorrect things to him and about God. And in the end of the story, Job is victorious!

Victory Journal

Jesus paid the price for curses so we can receive the blessings. Take a minute to thank God.

Dear God,

Thank you for the people in my life who I love and who love me. I am richly blessed! And thank you for all those things that were taken away. The losses hurt, and I don't necessarily like them, but I trust that you can use it all for good. Please help me to learn from my losses and not cling to them. Help me to celebrate those I love every day.

Amen.

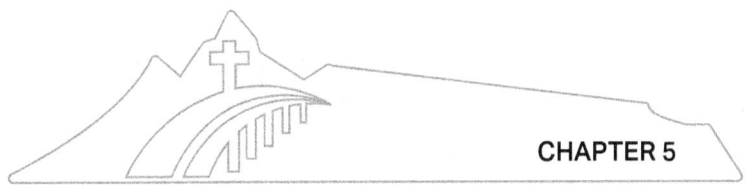

CHAPTER 5

Looking for Love

> *"But God showed his great love for us by sending Christ to die for us while we were still sinners."* (Romans 5:8 NLT)

In Chapter 5 of my book *Change Course*, I share the stories of my marriages and divorces. This was a hard chapter to write because the failures were put on pages for everyone to see. But it was important for me to be real so that other people can find healing and love after their own challenges, mistakes, and sins.

As I mentioned in my story, I was haunted by my sin and mistakes for many years. I spent a long time looking for love and acceptance from the wrong kind of men, and found it hard to feel worthy of love, especially God's love. But in my healing journey, I came to find

Victory Journal

out that God loved me through my mistakes. Accepting God's unconditional love, allowed me to finally receive love from my husband Jim.

Maybe you've made some mistakes in relationships with others and have been haunted by your own past sins, feeling unloved by God. Don't worry, there was hope for me, so there is hope for you too.

In this chapter of the book, you'll identify crucial relationships in your life, look for behavior patterns, and notice where you might be looking for love in the wrong places instead of accepting God's love for you.

Looking for Love

EXERCISES

Make a list of all the crucial male relationships in your life. This can include a father, brother, boyfriend, friend, mentor, spouse, or any others. These are men who either loved you or you loved them. (Change this to female relationships if you are a man reading this.)

Victory Journal

Go back to your list and underline all the negative relationships. (Those who mistreated you, abused you, or didn't value you or your contributions to the relationship.)

How did these people make you feel about yourself?

When you look at the names of the people you underlined, what were you hoping to receive from them in return for your love?

Looking for Love

Why didn't you receive what you were hoping for?

Were there poor decisions or mistakes you made when you didn't receive what you were looking for? What were they?

Victory Journal

Now go back to your list and circle all the names of people who impacted you positively. (Those who made you feel safe, loved, valued, and respected.)

When you look at the names of the people you circled, what was it that you received from them?

Were there good or wise decisions you made because of how these people loved and cared for you? What were they?

Looking for Love

Are there relationship mistakes you made that you are still feeling guilty about? Why or why not?

If you knew God loved you unconditionally, would that change the type of person you choose to have key relationships with? Why or why not?

What steps can you take to discover and accept God's forgiveness and love for you?

Victory Journal

BEYOND THE FINISH LINE

There are levels to explore in our relationships. If you want to go deeper, continue the exercise from this chapter with more of your crucial relationships adding more details to your answers.

Looking for Love

GOD'S LOVE

The fact that God loves us unconditionally may seem hard to accept, especially if none of our human relationships had that kind of love in them. It's also hard to accept if you are carrying the weight of unforgiveness on your back. Take a minute to talk to God about it.

Dear God,

I have a hard time believing you would love me when I have been hurt and unloved by people. I don't understand your unconditional love, but I accept it. Thank you for loving me despite myself and my mistakes. I am tired of carrying guilt and shame around. I bring it to you, lay it at your feet Lord, and ask you, to forgive me.

Thank you! Amen.

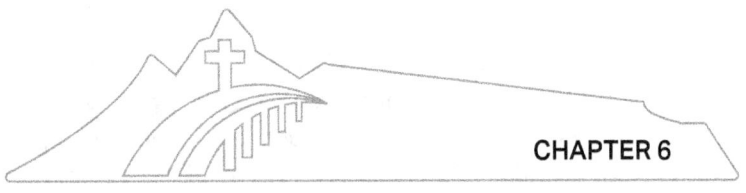

CHAPTER 6

Parenting Joys

> *"There's no way to be a perfect mother and a million ways to be a good one."*
> *– Jill Churchill*

In Chapter 6 of my book *Change Course*, I reflect on motherhood as my favorite occupation. If it were any other occupation, I may have been fired based on my poor performance. Yet, I believe mothers are trying to do the best they can. Both my girls are grown now and are mothers, so I got a promotion to grandmother. It may seem like there is a mother competition and pressure to be perfect these days and the joy of motherhood sometimes gets lost in chaos.

In this chapter, if you are a mother, you will go through an exercise to recount some of the joys of your

Victory Journal

motherhood experience and release your regrets over your mistakes. If you are not a mother either by choice or circumstance, take these questions to your mother (or who was a mother figure for you) and ask her to answer them for you. You'll learn something about your mother (or mother figure) and yourself in the process. If your mother is not available to do this, write her a note thanking her for being your mother and sharing one fond memory you have from your childhood.

Parenting Joys

EXERCISES

Looking back on some of your early motherhood days, for each of your children, list one of your biggest joys or one of the smallest moments that made you glad you were their mother. (If you are a male and a father, change the context to fit you.)

For each of your children, write out your hopes and dreams for them today. (No matter how old they are.)

Victory Journal

What is one thing you know now that you want to tell your younger self about parenting?

List one moment when you felt like you "blew it" as a parent.

Holding onto regrets can keep you from living the life you want. Write out a note to yourself forgiving yourself and releasing any regret you feel.

Parenting Joys

If you could say anything encouraging to a mother of little ones today, what would it be?

Set a goal to send the joy of parenting you wrote down to each of your children. If your child is not available to do this with, you can still write it out and share it with a friend.

Victory Journal

BEYOND THE FINISH LINE
If you want to go deeper in this exercise, reach out to a close friend who is a mother and go through these exercises with her to help her remember joy and release regrets.

Parenting Joys

GOD'S LOVE FOR YOUR CHILDREN

God gives children to us as a gift, but they belonged to Him before they became ours. Take a minute to thank God for your children (and/or your mother) and release them to Him.

Dear God,

Thank you for giving me the gift of my children (and/or my mother) and the gift of motherhood (or fatherhood). I can see your unconditional love for me in the way I unconditionally love my children. I only want what's best for them, and what's best for them is you. I release my children to you and ask you to make yourself and your love known to them.

Amen.

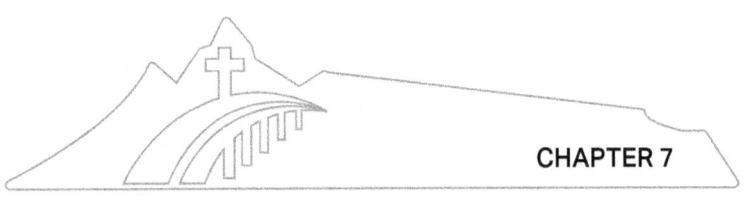

CHAPTER 7

Health & Addiction: Choosing Life

"The temptations in your life are no different from what others experience. And God is faithful. He will not allow the temptation to be more than you can stand. When you are tempted, he will show you a way out so that you can endure." (1 Corinthians 10:13 NLT)

In my book *Change Course*, I share about my husband's struggle with an addiction to alcohol. And I also share my stepdad's and my struggle with addiction to sugar. Then my journey to good health, or energy as I like to call it. Energy to live out my heart's desire.

Addiction comes in many forms and sizes. We are familiar with addiction to alcohol and drugs, but we often skip over addictions to sugar, salt, food, exercise, shopping, gambling, pornography, social media, work, and unfortunately, the list goes on.

In this chapter of the book, you will identify any addictive behaviors you might have and reflect on how you can get energy and strength for the life you want to live.

EXERCISES

What is one thing you consistently do when you are stressed out or anxious?

What do you consistently turn to when you want to numb feelings of pain, loss, or failure?

What behaviors do you engage in consistently when you are bored or lonely?

Do you now, or have you in the past, struggled with an addiction to anything? If so, what is it?

Victory Journal

How do/did you feel when you engaged in that addiction?

_____

_____

_____

How do/did you feel when you couldn't engage in that addiction?

_____

_____

_____

Does addictive behavior hinder you from living the life you want? Circle one:

True or False

Are you willing to stop the addictive behavior and/or get professional help so you can change course? Circle one:

Yes or No

Health & Addiction: Choosing Life

What changes will you need to make to get the health (a.k.a. energy) you need to change course and live the life you want?

_____

_____

_____

_____

Set a goal to start making some changes to replace addiction with positive energy.

It may be to tell a friend, or call a counselor or coach, turn your phone off at 7 pm tonight, drink 3 additional glasses of water tomorrow, cancel that Amazon order you placed today, or read the Bible daily.

Pick one step and write it below.

_____

_____

_____

Victory Journal

BEYOND THE FINISH LINE

If you are just starting this journey to change course on addiction and health, let me tell you that this is a lifelong journey (I am still a work in-progress), one you will need to be intentional about daily. But the prize is worth it! Don't stop at your one step. After you complete that one, set another step and another until all those steps add up to a giant leap forward.

Health & Addiction: Choosing Life

GOD'S HELP

One thing my husband Jim taught me, is that when he wants to drink alcohol, he must turn it over to God. Take a minute to turn the addictions and health concerns over to God. He's great at listening and helping us!

Dear God,

I am struggling with an addiction to

_____.

I need your help. I know I need to make some changes if I am going to change course and live the fullest life you have for me. Please help me to keep taking steps, one at a time.

Thank you for your grace and love.

Amen

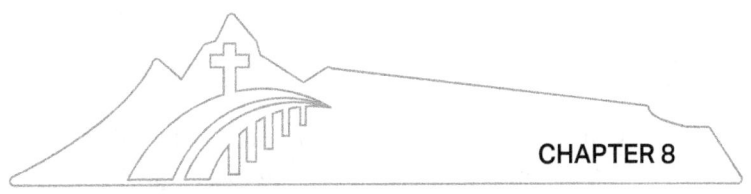

CHAPTER 8

Believing is Seeing

> *"Call to me and I will answer you. I'll tell you marvelous and wondrous things that you could never figure out on your own."*
> (Jeremiah 33:3 MSG)

In Chapter 8 of my book *Change Course*, I share my faith journey with God. I share my childhood faith, spurred on by my mother; my years of being far from God; my time as a "convenient Christian"; and the deepening of my faith through the years. I also share my physical healing experiences with God's glory light, twice in my life.

Maybe you can relate to some of my experiences, maybe you can't. Either way, God wants to have a relationship with everyone, and since He made us all individually, that relationship is going to be unique for you.

I don't know where you are at in your relationship with God, or your journey of faith, but this chapter of the book will give you a chance to explore that, even if it's something you haven't paid much attention to until now. Maybe you aren't ready to go down that road right now and you need to come back to this chapter later, that's okay. We are made of both physical and spiritual beings and the renewed spiritual side of your life will add fullness and joy to your heart's desire that you want to live.

Believing is Seeing

EXERCISES
What are your earliest memories around God and faith?

Did you have anyone in your early life who encouraged you to seek God? Who was it, and how did they guide your faith?

Did you ever go through a period in your life when you felt far away from God? Describe that time in your life.

Victory Journal

Did you ever go through a period in your life when you felt especially close to God? Describe that time in your life.

_____

_____

_____

_____

If God was sitting next to you right now, what would you say to Him?

_____

_____

_____

_____

Believing is Seeing

God is always speaking to us, but we aren't always listening. He speaks in multiple ways, but one way is through His word, the Holy Bible. Read the following verses from God's word and answer the questions for reflection below each one.

> *"For I know the plans I have for you," declares the Lord, "plans to prosper you and not to harm you, plans to give you hope and a future."*
> (Jeremiah 29:11 NIV)

What do you hear God speaking to you personally as you read this declaration from Him?

_____

_____

_____

_____

Victory Journal

> *"Look! I stand at the door and knock. If you hear my voice and open the door, I will come in, and we will share a meal together as friends."* (Revelation 3:20 NLT)

What do you hear God speaking to you personally as you read this invitation from Him?

_____

_____

_____

_____

_____

Believing is Seeing

> *"For the hearts of these people are hardened, and their ears cannot hear, and they have closed their eyes— so their eyes cannot see, and their ears cannot hear, and their hearts cannot understand, and they cannot turn to me and let me heal them."* (Matthew 13:15 NLT)

What do you hear God saying to you personally as He shares His heart?

_____

_____

_____

_____

_____

Hearing God takes practice and quiet time. Set a goal to listening to God once a day (later you will find you talk and hear God all day long as you would a dear friend). You can try a verse exercise like the one above and then listen to how God speaks to your heart.

Victory Journal

BEYOND THE FINISH LINE

Wherever you are in your faith journey, there is always room to go deeper. Being around other people on a similar faith journey helped my faith grow. I encourage you to find a faith community class about God or the Bible that you can take with other people.

Believing is Seeing

GOD'S DESIRE

God desires to have a relationship with you, but you decide how deep it goes and if it grows. Seek Him and take a minute to talk to God about your desires. He is always ready and waiting with open arms.

Dear God,

When I think about the fact that you love me, I feel overwhelmed and unworthy, but I thank you for your love. Thank you for being with me throughout my life, even when I was distant and didn't want to spend time with you. I am thankful you want to have a relationship with me. I want to have one with you and go deeper with you. I want to learn to listen when you speak and see you work in my life.

Amen.

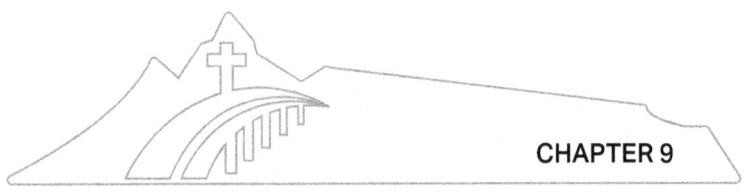

CHAPTER 9

Finding Purpose and Dreaming Again

"Take delight in the LORD, and he will give you your heart's desires." (Psalm 37:4 NLT)

In chapter 9 of my book *Change Course*, I share various dreams I've had and how some went the way I had hoped they would, and others didn't. I cataloged my career progression, my modeling dreams and businesses that succeeded and others that didn't go as planned. Each step along the way, I learned to keep dreaming and keep trying.

In this chapter of the book, you will get to revisit your dreams, and spark some new dreams for your life, and the things you want to accomplish.

Victory Journal

EXERCISES

What is something that you always wanted to do when you were younger?

_____

_____

If money were no object, what would you do with your time?

_____

_____

What needs or causes do you care most about?

_____

_____

What have you always been good at?

_____

_____

Finding Purpose and Dreaming Again

Who do you admire the most? And why?

Think of a time when you felt fulfilled, satisfied, or most alive; what were you doing at that time?

Based on your answers above, what are three dreams you would like to have or accomplish or experience in the new life you are creating as you change course?

Victory Journal

Sometimes we don't accomplish our dreams and change course in our lives because it looks too big and scary to accomplish.

What is one thing you can do this week to start moving towards your dreams and the new life you want? (Example: Find someone who has already accomplished what you want to do and set up time to talk to them about how they did it.)

Finding Purpose and Dreaming Again

BEYOND THE FINISH LINE

This is only the beginning of the new life you want. Keep breaking your dreams into small steps until you accomplish them. Don't give up! And don't let things distract you and other people derail you. Keep moving towards what you want, even if it takes you outside your comfort zone. You are transforming your life and it's worth the hard work.

Victory Journal

GOD'S DREAM AND OUR HEART'S DESIRE

I believe God puts dreams in our hearts because He wants us to accomplish the plans and purposes He has for our lives. As we take steps towards our dreams and desires, God helps us along the way. Take a minute to tell God about your dreams and ask for His guidance.

Dear God,

I have a dream to

_____.

This dream is both scary and exciting to me. I believe you put this dream and desire on my heart because you have good plans and purposes for me. Please direct my steps, give me wisdom, and help me along the way so I can see your plans for me come to pass.

Amen.

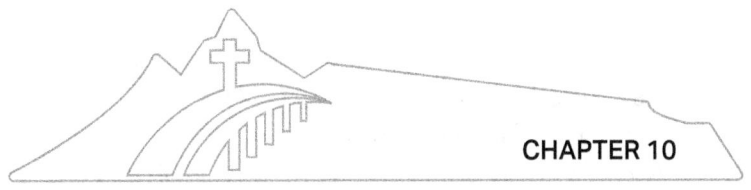

CHAPTER 10

Embracing Adventure

> *Jesus said: "The thief's purpose is to steal and kill and destroy. My purpose is to give them a rich and satisfying life."* (John 10:10 NLT)

In Chapter 10 of my book *Change Course*, I share my passion and joy for racing, one of the dreams that came true for me. I also talk about the dreams of writing that book and my dreams of speaking to others about what I've learned.

None of these things were easy, but they were all adventures for me. Trying new things is how we change course and create the life we want, living out our heart's desire. And in that, we find joy in living a full life.

Victory Journal

In this chapter of the book, you will identify adventures (a.k.a. new things) that you would like to try. They might be part of your dreams from the previous chapter, or they might be something completely different.

Embracing Adventure

EXERCISES

The definition of an adventure is an exciting or unusual experience that usually involves risks.

Based on that definition, list three things you would consider to be an "adventure" that you would like to try. It can be taking a college class or going skydiving. It just needs to be something that challenges you to move outside your comfort zone.

1. _____
2. _____
3. _____

Why do you want to try those things?

_____

_____

_____

How do each of these move you outside your comfort zone?

_____

_____

_____

Victory Journal

Take the adventure you want to try first and make a list of the steps you would need to experience it.

How would this adventure bring joy to your life?

Would this adventure increase your confidence to try other adventures? Why or why not?

This week do the first thing on your list of steps to experience your adventure.

Embracing Adventure

BEYOND THE FINISH LINE

Once you complete your first adventure, write down your experience below.

Now select another adventure from your list and use the same process and go after it!

Victory Journal

GOD'S JOY

God wants to see us enjoy life to the fullest. Part of that includes taking risks and trying new things. Take a minute to tell God about the adventures you want to take. Ask Him to give you the courage to follow through with His help.

Dear God,

I desire to go on an adventure where I

_____.

Thank you for wanting to give me joy in this life.

Please help me to move outside my comfort zone and enjoy the ride!

Amen.

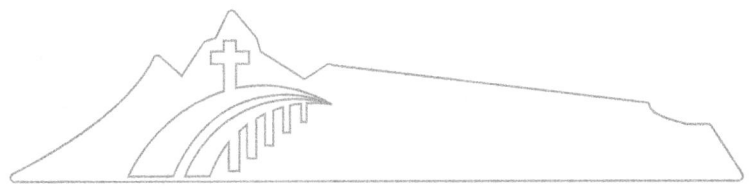

Conclusion

You did it! You completed the exercises to live out your heart's desire and experience the purpose God has for you. You've made a lot of progress and changes throughout this book. How will you celebrate your victories?

This is only the beginning. This isn't a race to see who can get to the finish line the fastest (unless your adventure is on the racetrack), this is a journey to get to the life you want, your heart's desire. To do that, you might need to come back and revisit this book. Do that as often as you need so you can continue to change course and live the life you desire.

Keep your pedal to the metal and don't let anything stop you! You're worth it!

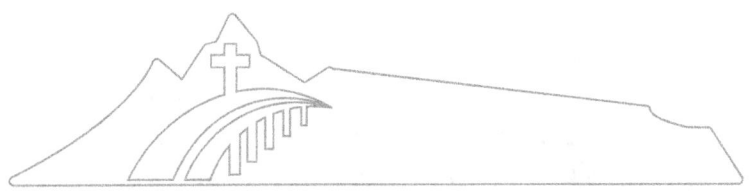

Author's note to all readers

For me the ultimate life changing event was when I received God's Son, Jesus Christ, as my Lord and Savior. And then was filled with God's Spirit (a.k.a. Holy Spirit) to guide me in this new Christian life.

If you don't know God the Father, God the Son (Jesus Christ), and God the Holy Spirit yet, please read the Holy Bible (my favorite translations are NIV and NLT).

You can also grab a copy of my devotional, *Rooted in Jesus,* to learn more.

How to receive Jesus and His beautiful love and grace? Start by saying the following prayer with all your heart:

Victory Journal

Lord Jesus, I confess I have sinned against you and people, forgive me, I am sorry from the depth of my being. I believe you are the Son of God, was crucified, died, buried, and was raised from the dead for my justification so that I could be right standing before you. I believe your blood has washed away my sins, never to be seen again, and I am cleansed. I ask you to show me who I am in you; my identity in you.

*Help me to grow my roots deep into you and help me understand the depth of your love for me. I trust you with my life now and for all eternity. I put my faith in your shed blood, Jesus. Right now, rescue me, heal me, deliver me, and set me free.
I thank you Jesus.*

I invite the Holy Spirit right now to baptize me with His presence and His person. You said in your Word you would never deny anyone who asks for the gift of the Holy Spirit. I am asking now, Holy Spirit come upon me now, with the glorious evidence of speaking in tongues. I desire your power and strength

Author's note to all readers

to live a Christian life with meaning and purpose all for the glory of God. In Jesus' name.

Amen

Now join a good bible-based church and continue to seek Jesus with all your heart! *"But thanks be to God! He gives us the victory through our Lord Jesus Christ."* (1Corinthians 15:57 NIV)

TOGETHER WE ARE VICTORIOUS THROUGH JESUS!

As I live in this earthly world and not yet perfected by Christ Jesus, I am a work in progress. I have come a long way on my journey, and I intend to always try and improve myself and embrace all that God has for me.

It has been helpful for me to understand that God created us all as a three part being/person. We are first and foremost, a spirit. We have a soul, which is our mind, will, and emotions. And we live in a body of flesh. We are comprised of Spirit, Soul, and Body.

The nature of the exercises contained in this book dealt mainly with healing your soul (mind, will, and emotions) except for the chapter on additions and health which dealt most likely with the soul and body. If after you went through the exercises, you identify that you need some additional professional help to process what you are experiencing, do not feel condemned if that is the case.

You may also feel like you are controlled by forces beyond your control and are demonic and oppressive in nature. As you read through the New Testament of the Bible you read that Jesus spent a third of His ministry on casting out evil spirits. So, do not feel condemned if you need additional help. Seek out and consult with a trained Christian deliverance minister for the next steps to obtain your freedom.

Paul, the Apostle to the gentiles, wrote a letter to the believers in Ephesus. And in Chapter 6 verses 10–18 of this letter, we find the following wise words that are very helpful and needed for today:

> *"Finally, be strong in the Lord and in his mighty power.*
>
> *Put on the full armor of God, so that you can take your stand against the devil's schemes.*
>
> *For our struggle is not against flesh and blood, but against the rulers, against the authorities, against the powers of this dark*

Author's note to all readers

world and against the spiritual forces of evil in the heavenly realms.

Therefore put on the full armor of God, so that when the day of evil comes, you may be able to stand your ground, and after you have done everything, to stand.

Stand firm then, with the belt of truth buckled around your waist, with the breastplate of righteousness in place, and with your feet fitted with the readiness that comes from the gospel of peace.

In addition to all this, take up the shield of faith, with which you can extinguish all the flaming arrows of the evil one.

Take the helmet of salvation and the sword of the Spirit, which is the word of God.

And pray in the Spirit on all occasions with all kinds of prayers and requests. With this in mind, be alert and always keep on praying for all the Lord's people."
(Ephesians 6:10–18 NIV)

Victory Journal

In my own life God has opened my spiritual eyes so I could see into the "unseen" spiritual realm and "see" with my spiritual discernment eyes the evil demons that were attacking me, so I could better understand, and combat them. Satan and his demons are real whether we like to acknowledge them or not. Do not be frightened by them, like I was previously, but be aware of them and take action to eliminate them from your life. Pray to God for strength and discernment so can understand the full situation and act as needed with the authority given to us by Christ Jesus. (See Matthew 28:18–20, Mark 16:17–18, Luke 10:19–20)

With the good shepherd, Jesus, we have HOPE and VICTORY.

"Therefore Jesus said again, 'Very truly I tell you, I am the gate for the sheep.

All who have come before me are thieves and robbers, but the sheep have not listened to them.

I am the gate; whoever enters through me will be saved. They will come in and go out, and find pasture.

Author's note to all readers

> *The thief comes only to steal and kill and destroy; I have come that they may have life, and have it to the full.*
>
> *I am the good shepherd. The good shepherd lays down his life for the sheep.'"* (John 10:7–11 NIV)

You are worth the time and effort it takes to get you to a place of joy, peace, and freedom so you can live out your heart's desire in Victory.

Love to you today and every day.

Leslie Jackson

www.ingramcontent.com/pod-product-compliance
Lightning Source LLC
Chambersburg PA
CBHW052150070526
44585CB00017B/2053